Ballerina Paper Dolls

Coloring & Craft Book

Written and Illustrated by Vanessa Salgado

ISBN: 979-8-9868612-3-4
www.Crafterina.com

Let's make

Ballerina Paper Dolls

Create your very own set of paper dolls with Crafterina!
Fun and easy to make, inside you'll find paper dolls,
outfits, accessories, backdrops, and a carrying case craft.
The back cover is also a craft with three adorable
ballerina paper dolls in full color.

Enjoy crafting and coloring paper dolls with your
family and friends from dance class!

For more dance and
paper doll fun:

www.Crafterina.com

Let's create

Ballerina Paper Dolls

Safety Note For Parents: All crafts require parent supervision to create.
There are pieces to cut out that will require your help. Have fun creating together!
Directions: Cut along the dotted line and connect the rectangle base to doll.

Stand Assembly:
Fold rectangle in half and
cut along dash lines.
Connect together
to stand upright.

Rectangle Paper Doll Stand ← Fold in half along the dotted line
Cut dash line →

Let's create

Ballerina Paper Dolls

Safety Note For Parents: All crafts require parent supervision to create.
There are pieces to cut out that will require your help. Have fun creating together!
Directions: Cut along the dotted line and connect the rectangle base to doll.

Stand Assembly:
Fold rectangle in half and
cut along dash lines.
Connect together
to stand upright.

Rectangle Paper Doll Stand   ← Fold in half along the dotted line
Cut dash line →

Let's create

Ballet Paper Dolls

Safety Note For Parents: All crafts require parent supervision to create.
There are pieces to cut out that will require your help. Have fun creating together!
Directions: Cut along the dotted line and connect the rectangle base to doll.

Stand Assembly:
Fold rectangle in half and
cut along dash lines.
Connect together
to stand upright.

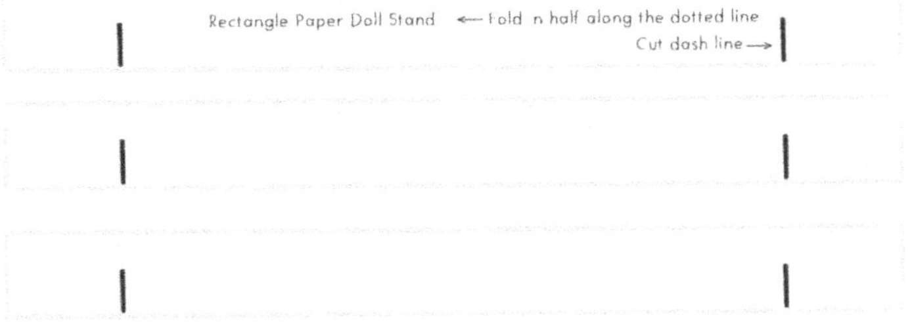

Rectangle Paper Doll Stand   ← Fold in half along the dotted line

Cut dash line →

Let's create

Ballet Paper Dolls

Safety Note For Parents: All crafts require parent supervision to create.
There are pieces to cut out that will require your help. Have fun creating together!
Directions: Cut along the dotted line and connect the rectangle base to doll.

Stand Assembly:
Fold rectangle in half and
cut along dash lines.
Connect together
to stand upright.

Rectangle Paper Doll Stand   ← Fold in half along the dotted line
Cut dash line →

www.Crafterina.com

Let's create
Crafterina Paper Dolls

Directions: Cut out outfits and accessories.
Fold rectangles to connect to paper doll.

Crayons

Paper Dolls

Paper Dolls

Crayons

Let's create
Nutcracker Paper Dolls

Directions: Cut out outfits and accessories.
Fold rectangles to connect to paper doll.

Let's create
Firebird Paper Dolls

Directions: Cut out outfits and accessories.
Fold rectangles to connect to paper doll.

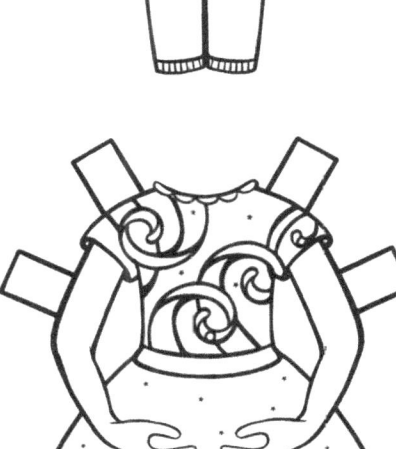

Let's create
Cinderella Paper Dolls

Directions: Cut out outfits and accessories.
Fold rectangles to connect to paper doll.

Let's create
Swan Lake Paper Dolls

Directions: Cut out outfits and accessories.
Fold rectangles to connect to paper doll.

Let's create
Sleeping Beauty Paper Dolls

Directions: Cut out outfits and accessories.
Fold rectangles to connect to paper doll.

Let's create crafts!

Paper Doll Tableau Directions:

1. Color and cut out template

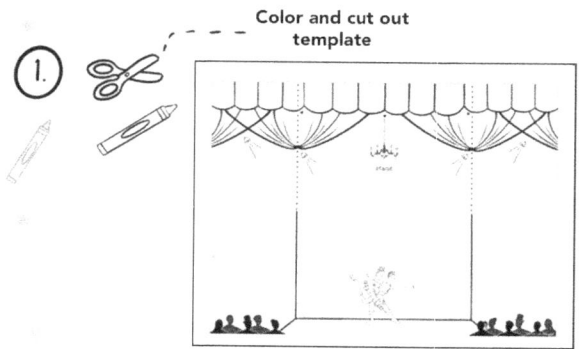

2. Fold along dotted lines to create 3D stand up tableau

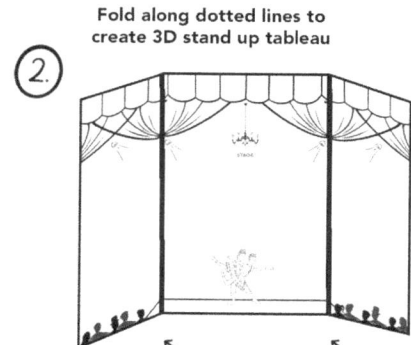

Paper Doll Carrying Case Directions:

1. Color and cut out template

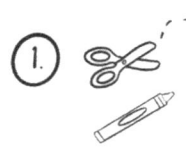

2. Fold in half along dotted line. Optional: use tape or glue to seal sides of case

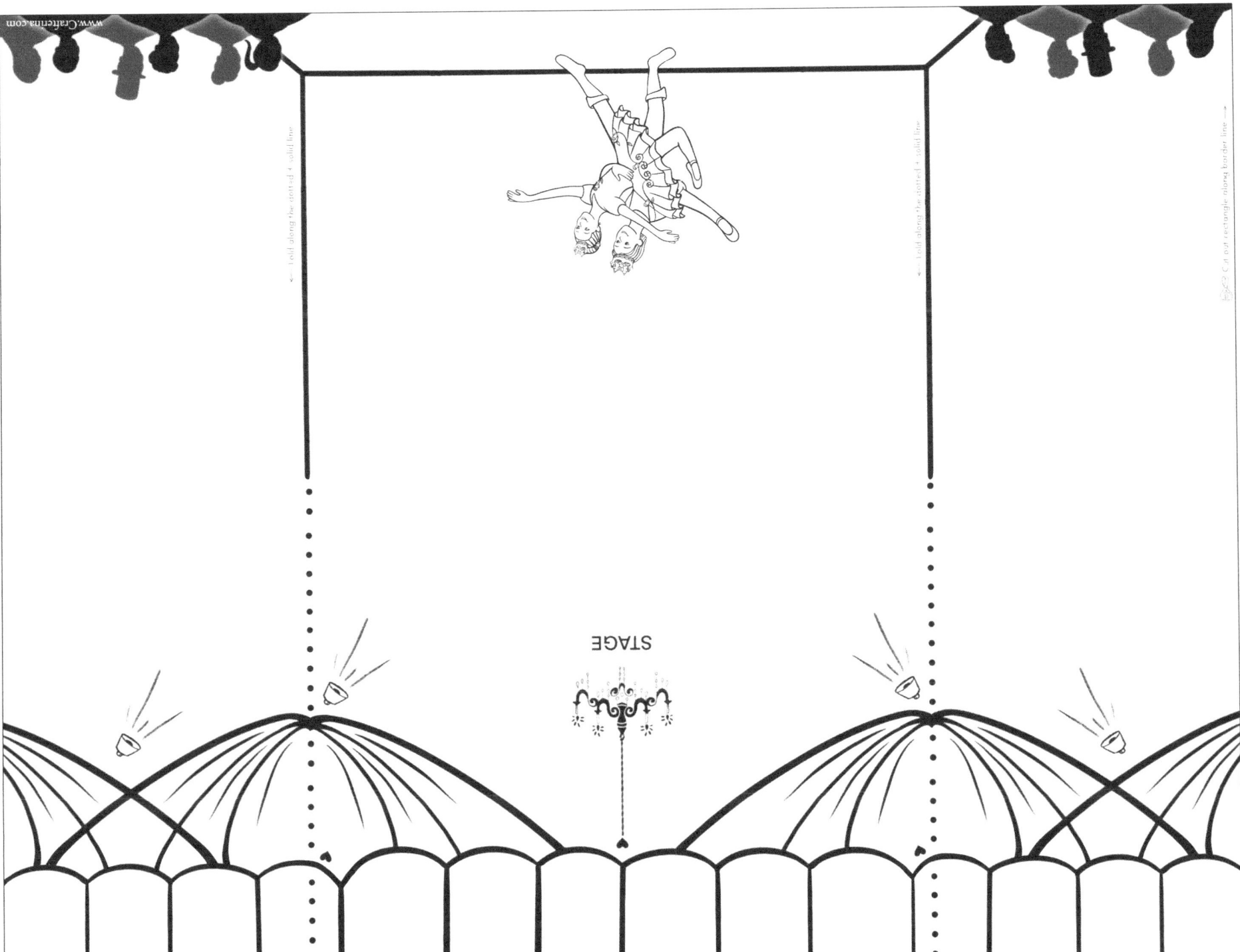

STAGE

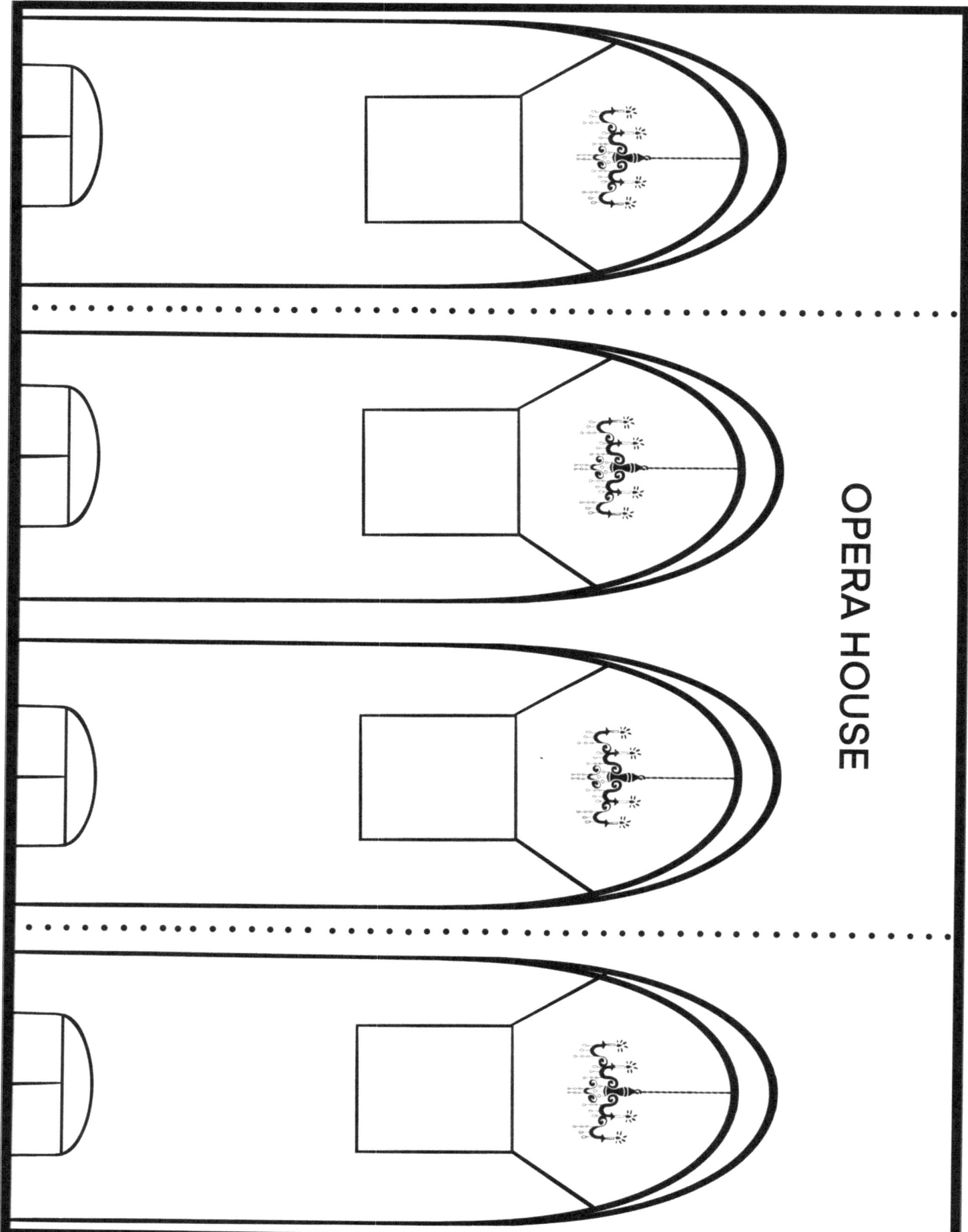

OPERA HOUSE

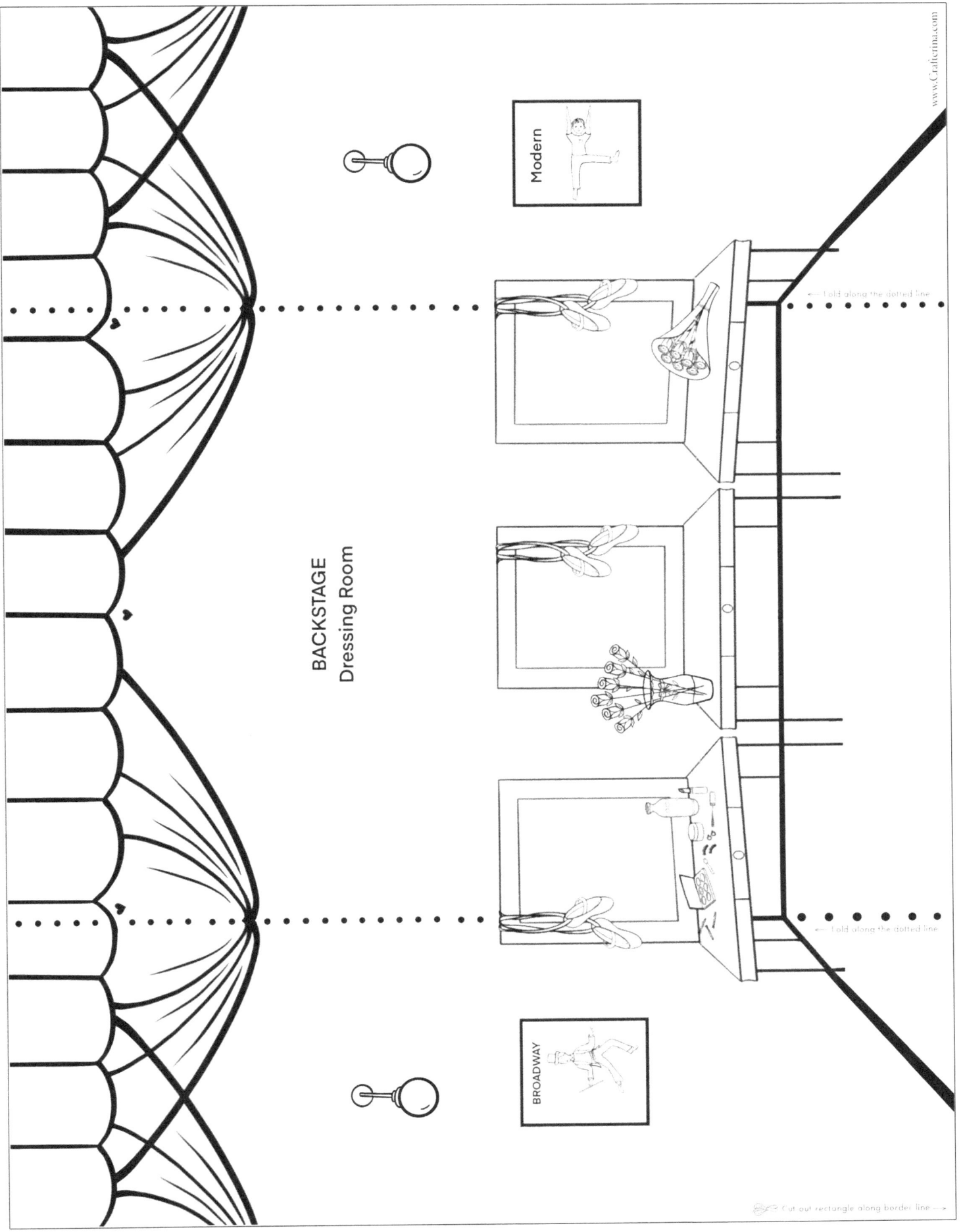

BACKSTAGE
Dressing Room

Modern

BROADWAY

← Fold along the dotted line

← Fold along the dotted line

Cut out rectangle along border line →

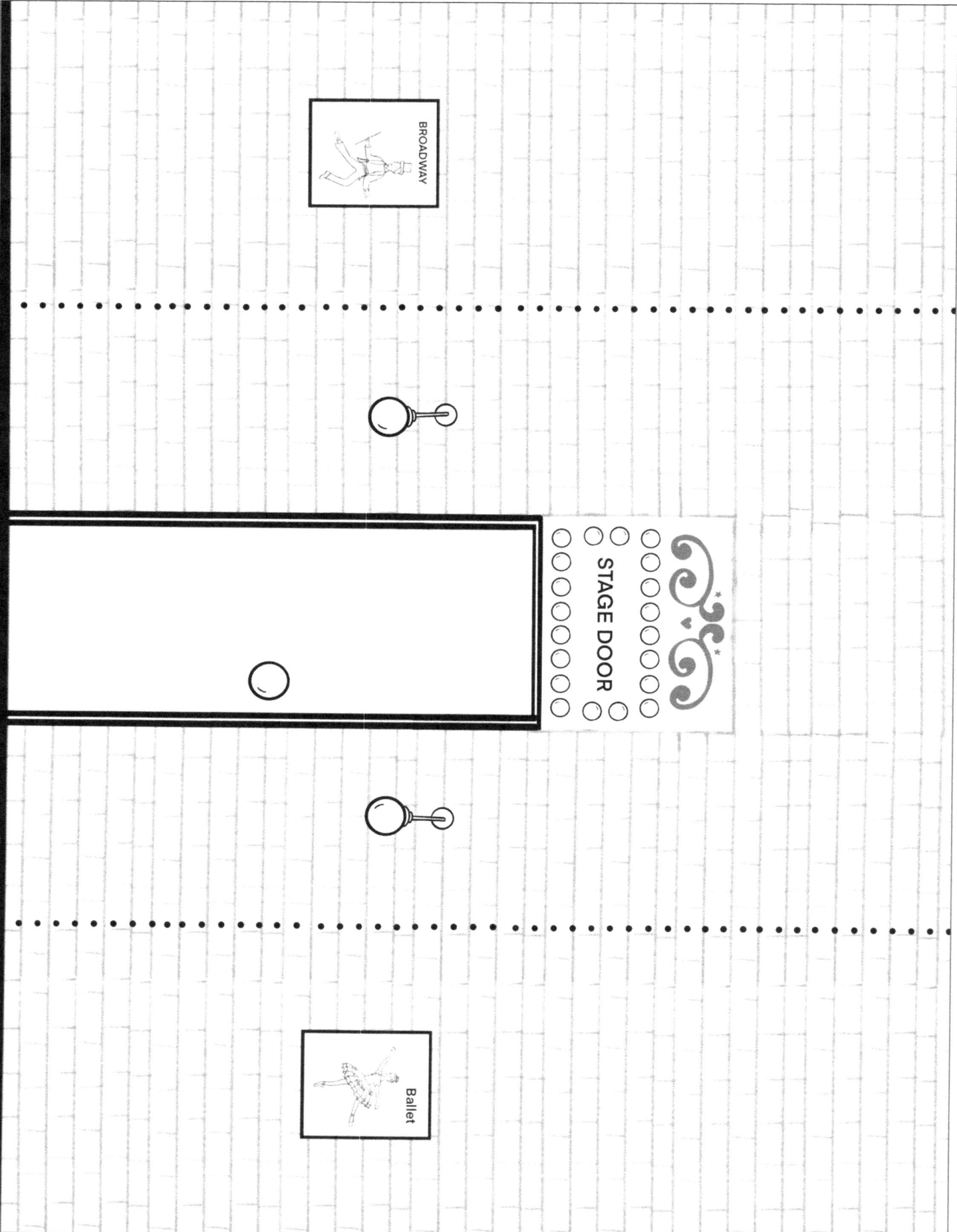

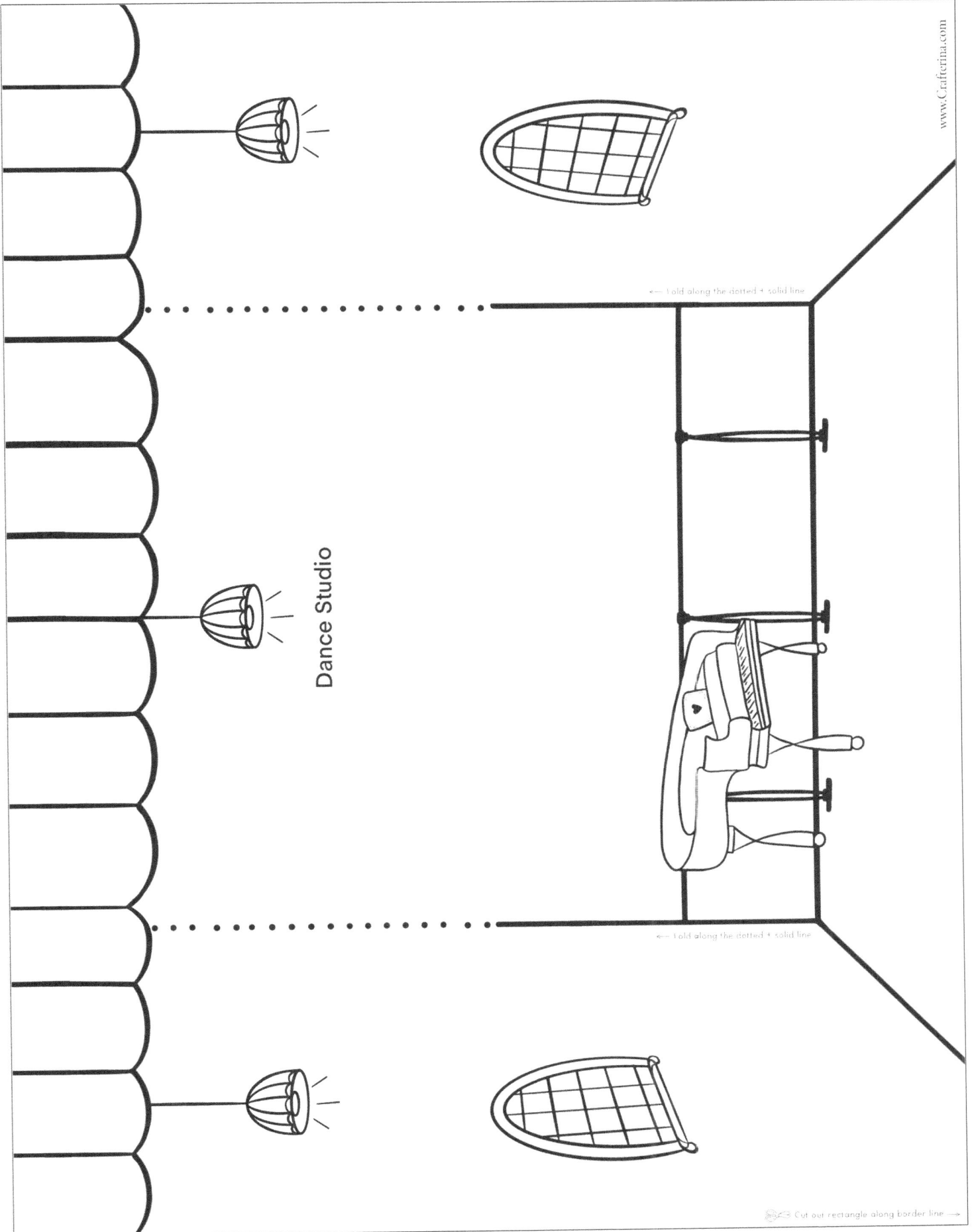

Dance Studio

← Fold along the dotted + solid line

← Fold along the dotted + solid line

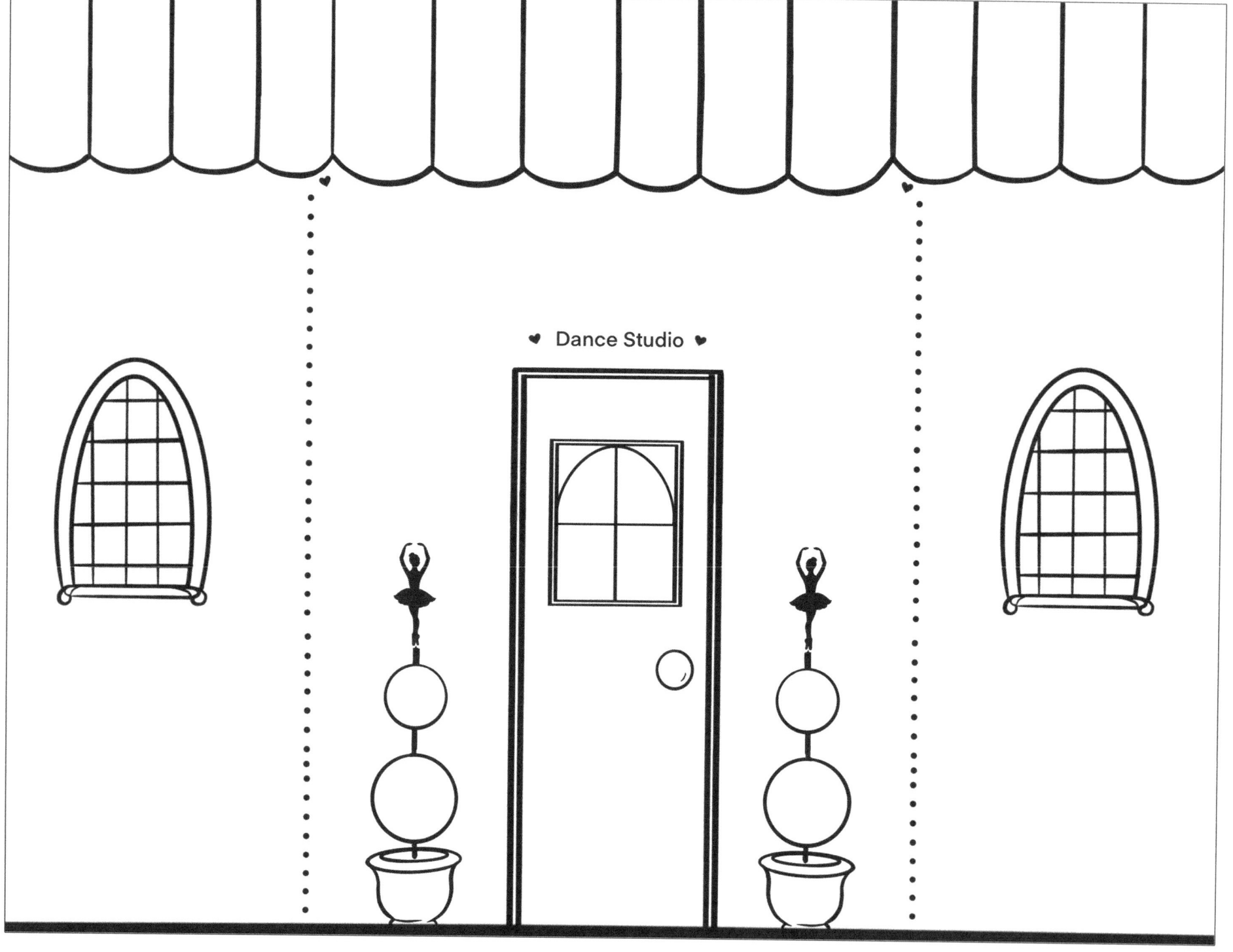

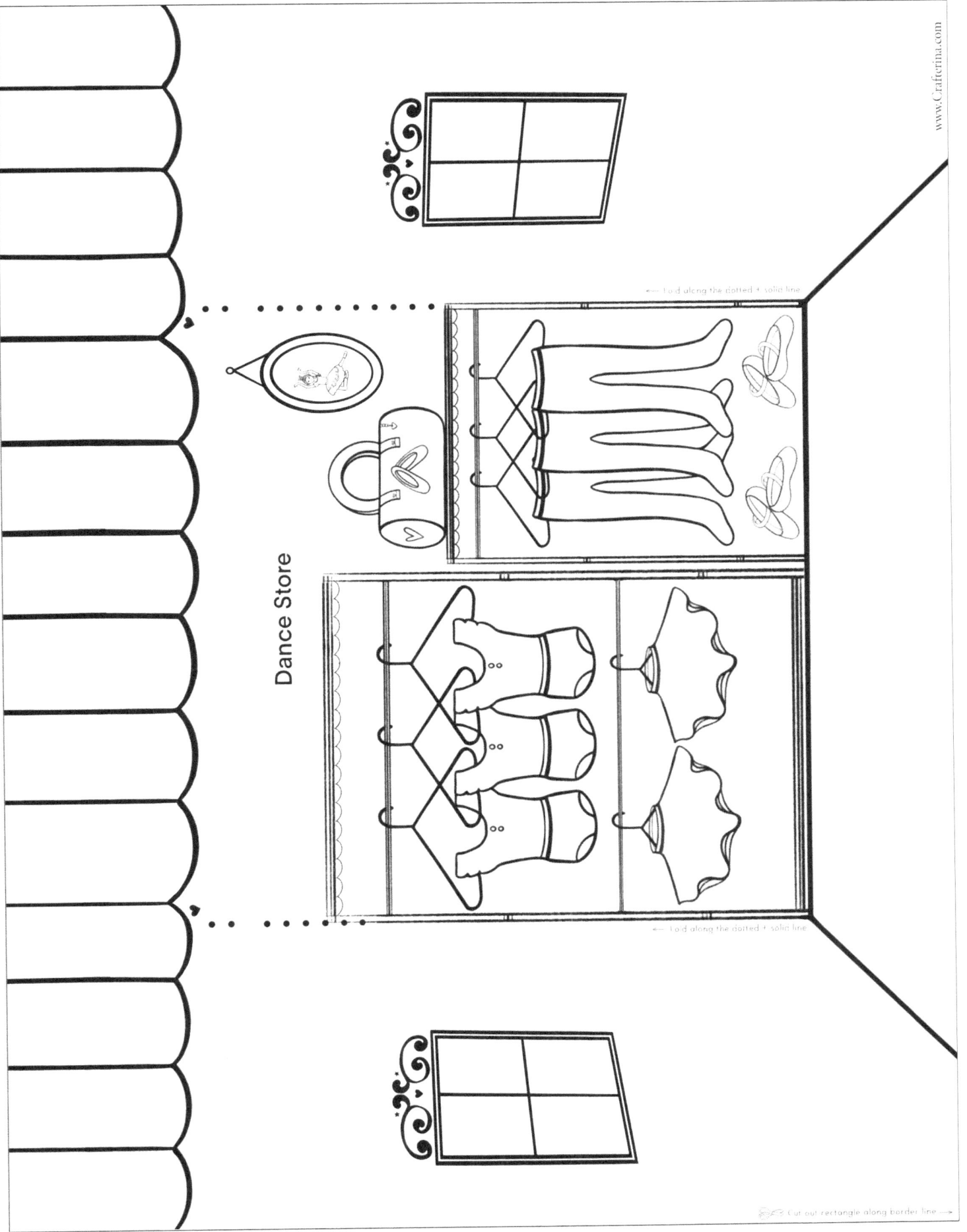

Dance Store

← Fold along the dotted + solid line

← Fold along the dotted + solid line

✂ Cut out rectangle along border line →

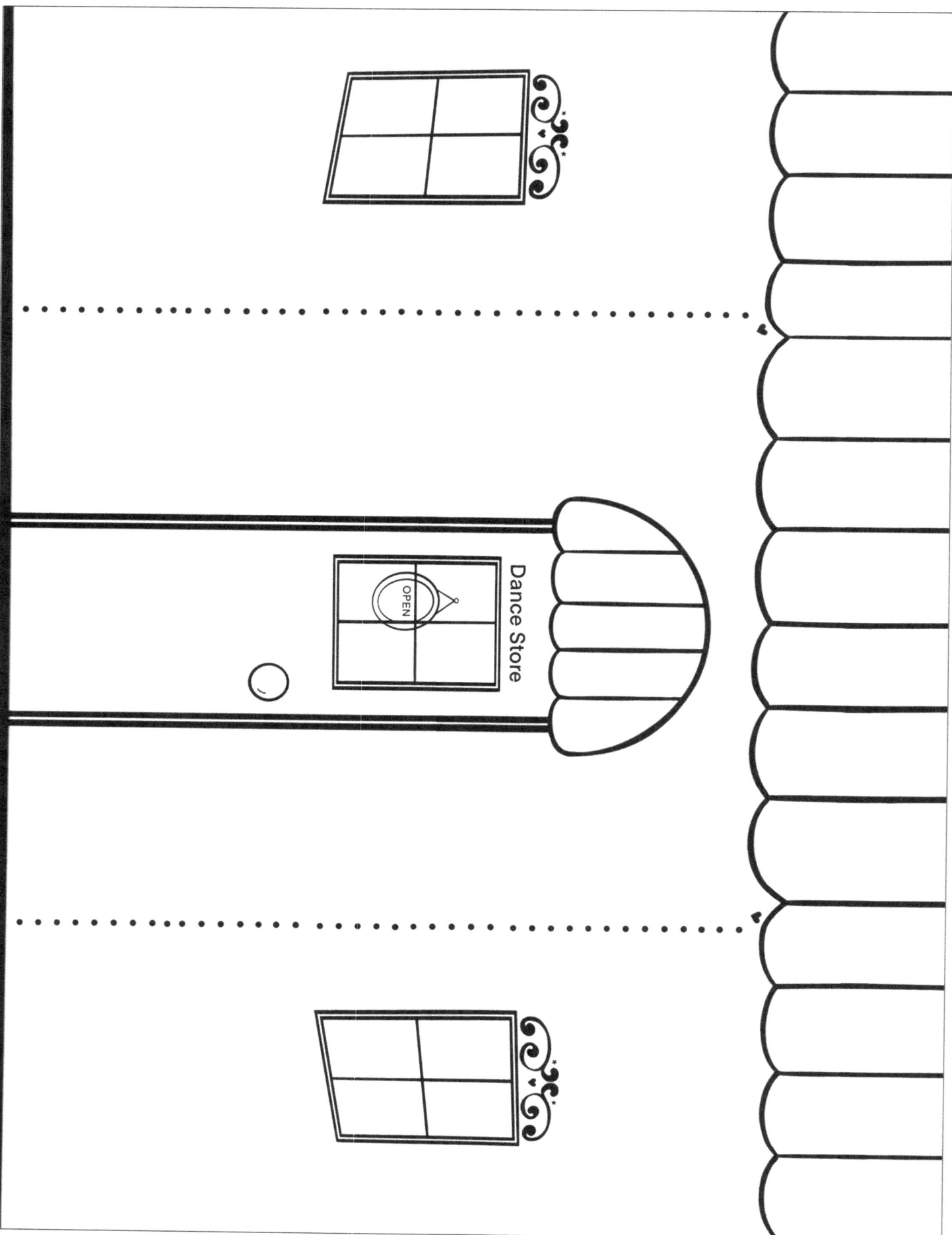

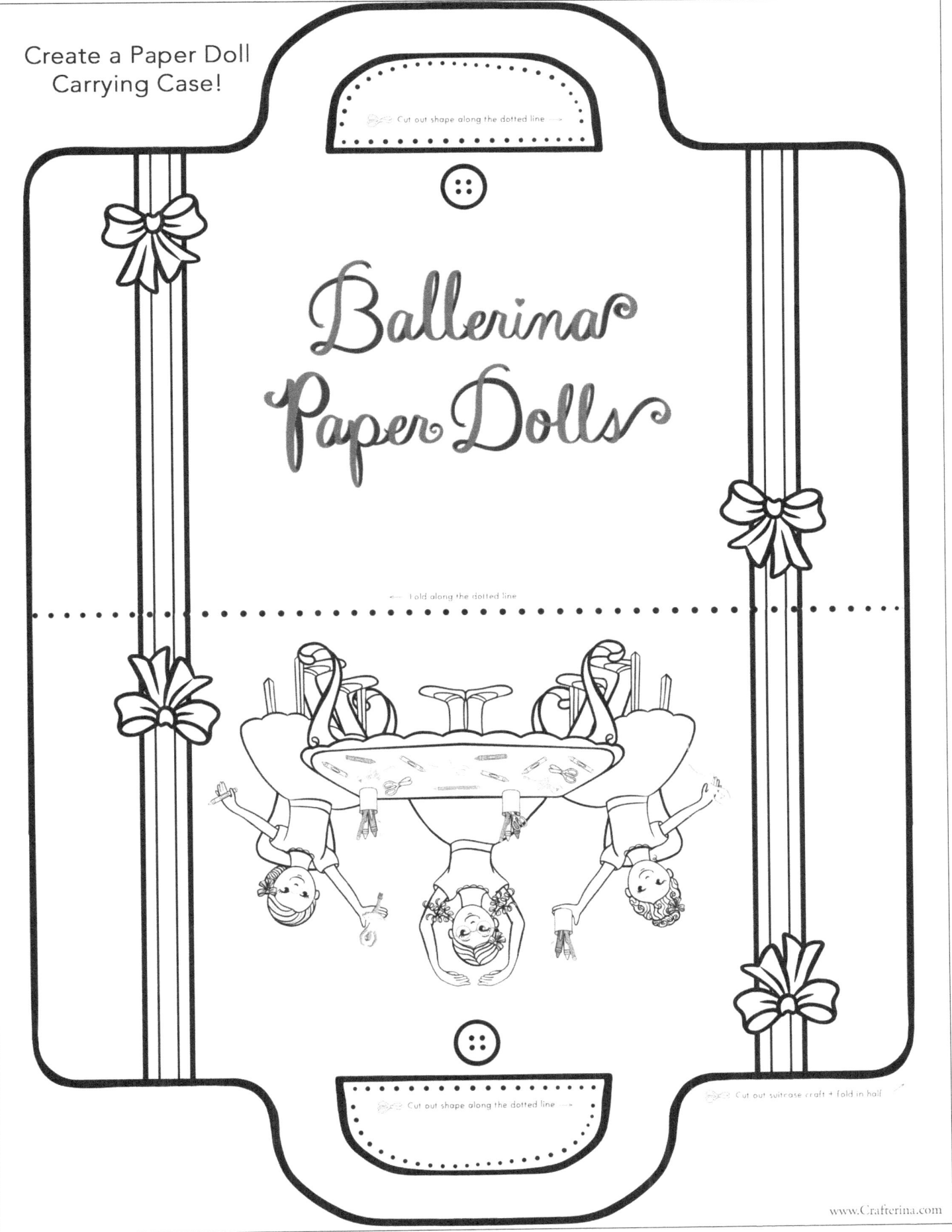

Create a Paper Doll
Carrying Case!

Cut out shape along the dotted line

Ballerina Paper Dolls

← Fold along the dotted line

Cut out shape along the dotted line →

Cut out suitcase craft + fold in half

About the Author

Vanessa Salgado is a Professional Dancer, Educator and Illustrator.

She has taught many little dancers across Manhattan, concentrating primarily at the Joffrey Ballet School, School at STEPS on Broadway, and Alvin Ailey School. She has also worked as an Associate for the Education Department at New York City Center. Vanessa is a graduate of the Alvin Ailey/Fordham University BFA Program at Lincoln Center and holds a certification in Dance Education. Her work has been featured in Dance Teacher Magazine, Dance Spirit, Dance Informa, and METRO US Newspaper, among others.

Her earliest memories involve story time with her dad, creating with her mom after school, and attending weekend ballet class alongside her sister, Donna. Her interests in visual art revealed themselves wholeheartedly in high school as she simultaneously trained for the professional dance world. As she transitioned into her college days and into her professional life, her incessant doodles and crafting have remained a source of wonder for all those around her.

For more information:
www.VanessaSalgado.com

About Crafterina®

Vanessa is also the creator of Crafterina® a series of dance education books and crafts for families. Designed to spark imagination and inspire movement at home, Crafterina® uniquely incorporates reading, creating and dancing in one. Through this interdisciplinary approach, Crafterina® playfully encourages empowerment and teaches youngsters they have the ability to make anything possible.

Inspire a lifelong love for learning in dance with the help of Crafterina®.

For more information, visit our website for books, crafts, and printables:

www.Crafterina.com